Read-Aloud Plays

EXPLORERS

by Jeannette Sanderson

SCHOLASTIC
PROFESSIONALBOOKS

NEW YORK   TORONTO   LONDON   AUCKLAND   SYDNEY
MEXICO CITY   NEW DELHI   HONG KONG   BUENOS AIRES

Scholastic Inc. grants teachers permission to photocopy the plays from this book for classroom use. No other part of this publication may be reproduced in whole or in part, or stored in a retrieval system, or transmitted in any form or by any means, electronic, mechanical, photocopying, recording, or otherwise, without written permission of the publisher. For information regarding permission, write to Scholastic Inc., 557 Broadway, New York, NY 10012.

Cover and interior design by Josué Castilleja
Cover illustration by Mona Mark
Interior illustrations by Tersea Southwell

ISBN 0-439-25181-8

1 2 3 4 5 6 7 8 9 10   40   01

CONTENTS

WEST OVER SEAS

Leif Eriksson and the Viking Discovery of America

CHARACTERS

NARRATOR

ERIK THE RED: father of Leif Eriksson

LEIF: Viking explorer, Leif Eriksson

THORVALD: brother of Leif

THORSTEIN: brother of Leif

BJARNI: a Viking merchant

VIKINGS 1 and 2: sailors on Leif Eriksson's voyage to America

TYRKIR: a German friend who sailed to America with Leif Eriksson

PROLOGUE

According to oral histories about Norse explorers passed down for generations, Leif Eriksson first heard about new lands over the "Western Ocean" from Bjarni Herjulfsson, a merchant who spotted them when he was blown off course while sailing from Iceland to Greenland. Eriksson, who the sagas say had the curiosity his fellow Norseman lacked, set sail to explore these unknown lands around 1000 A.D.

READ-ALOUD PLAYS: EXPLORERS Scholastic Professional Books

{ACT I}

Scene 1: Winter, about 1000 A.D. Bratahild, Greenland.

NARRATOR: Leif Eriksson had just returned home to Greenland from a trading voyage where he visited King Olaf Tryggvason of Norway. He had much to tell his father and brothers about his journey. And they had much to tell him.

ERIK THE RED: Welcome home, Son. You were away a long time.

LEIF: King Olaf bid me stay with him for a while. He was very kind and generous.

ERIK THE RED: As he should be to my son.

LEIF: He thanked you for your gifts and sent many in return.

ERIK THE RED: How was the trading?

LEIF: I made very good trades. In exchange for polar bear pelts, sealskins, and ivory, I returned with a shipload of wood, corn, and iron.

ERIK THE RED: I am glad, my son. We need all three.

THORVALD: Brother, how was the sailing?

LEIF: At times it was rough, but that is part of the adventure.

THORSTEIN: We heard of a most wonderful adventure while you were away.

LEIF: What was it?

THORSTEIN: Bjarni, son of Herjolf, sighted new lands across the Western Ocean.

ERIK THE RED: He found these new lands when blown off course while sailing from Iceland to Greenland.

LEIF: Did he explore these lands? What were they like?

NARRATOR: Leif's father and brothers shook their heads.

LEIF: Did he not explore them?

ERIK THE RED: He did not.

THORSTEIN: Bjarni was a fool.

THORVALD: He lacks curiosity. He did not even set foot on the lands. He can only describe what he saw from his ship.

LEIF: I cannot believe that. I must go and speak with Bjarni myself.

Scene 2: The following week. Herjolfsnes, Greenland.

NARRATOR: Leif wasted little time in going to speak with Bjarni, who had recently retired and was now living with his father.

BJARNI: Welcome, Leif. How was your voyage?

LEIF: It sounds dull compared to yours. Is it true that you have seen new lands in the Western Ocean?

BJARNI: Yes.

LEIF: Tell me what happened. What did you see?

NARRATOR: Bjarni pointed to a seat by the fire for Leif. Then he began to tell the story he liked to tell during the long winter nights of his retirement.

BJARNI: It was the winter of 986. I had returned to Iceland after a long trading voyage to spend the winter at my father's house. When I got there I learned he had sailed to Greenland with your father.

LEIF: So you decided to sail after him?

BJARNI: Yes. To some our voyage seemed foolhardy. Greenland was a new settlement then, and none of us had ever sailed the Greenland Sea. But I had planned to spend the winter with my father, and I was not going to let the unknown get in my way.

LEIF: A true Viking! But how did your journey go that you came to see these unknown lands?

BJARNI: Three days out of port, the ship was surrounded by fog. A north wind began driving us we could not see where. After many days the fog lifted. The sun came out again and we were able to get our bearings from the sky.

NARRATOR: Leif rubbed his hands together impatiently.

BJARNI: We hoisted sail again and sailed for a day and a night. Then we sighted land. When we drew near I could see that the country was wooded with low ridges. It had no mountains, no glaciers like the Greenland I had heard about.

LEIF: And you did not set foot on this new land?

BJARNI: No, I was looking for Greenland, for glaciers. So we kept sailing. Two days later we sighted another shore. When we got closer I saw there were no glaciers.

LEIF (*impatient*)**:** Who cares about glaciers! What was this land like?

BJARNI: It was flat and wooded.

LEIF: And still you did not stop?

BJARNI: No, though my crew asked me to. They wanted to stop for wood and water. But I told them we lacked for neither. Over their grumbling I instructed them to continue. With a southwesterly wind behind us, we sighted land again three days later.

LEIF: And it still was not Greenland?

BJARNI: No. It was an island, high and mountainous. And there were glaciers there. I told my men it looked good for nothing. We did not even lower our sail there, but continued sailing with a good southwesterly wind behind us. After four days and nights we sighted land for a fourth time.

LEIF: And?

BJARNI: I told my crew, "This looks like what I've been told about Greenland, so we'll make for land here." We did, and anchored on the very cape where my father lived, where I now live.

NARRATOR: Neither man spoke for a few minutes. Then Leif looked at Bjarni, questioningly.

LEIF: Did you ever want to go back and explore those lands?

BJARNI: No. I was a merchant. I did not have the vision of an explorer. But I think you do.

NARRATOR: Leif was deep in thought and did not hear what Bjarni had said. Then he looked up at the man, his eyes blazing.

LEIF: Will you sell me your ship?

BJARNI: I will. I have no more use for it.

LEIF: Good. It carried you and your men to these unknown lands. Maybe it will do the same for me.

⟪ ACT II ⟫

Scene 1: Summer, about 1001 A.D. Bratahild, Greenland.

NARRATOR: Leif readied the ship for the long journey. He put together a crew of Greenland's 35 best seamen. He had only one thing left to do—convince his father to lead the voyage.

LEIF: Father, I want you to lead this voyage as you led the voyage to Greenland.

ERIK THE RED: No. I am too old for such a journey. I can no longer do the work of a young man.

LEIF: All of Greenland looks to you as a leader. Who better to lead this voyage?

NARRATOR: Leif's father didn't answer.

LEIF: You are still the kinsman who is best at steering.

NARRATOR: Leif's father smiled.

ERIK THE RED: All right, if you really want me to, I will do it. It will be my last great adventure.

NARRATOR: The day they planned to set sail dawned bright and beautiful. Leif and his father set out on horseback for the short ride to the ship. Suddenly the horse Erik the Red was riding stumbled and Erik was thrown. Leif quickly got off his horse to help his father.

LEIF: Are you hurt?

ERIK THE RED: Only my foot.

LEIF: Can you still sail?

ERIK THE RED: I can, but I won't. This fall is a bad omen.

LEIF: Come father, you are so superstitious with your gods and your omens.

NARRATOR: But Erik refused to get up and sat where he had landed, shaking his head.

ERIK THE RED: It doesn't look as if I shall find any more countries; we shan't be able to go any further together.

LEIF: Stay if you wish, Father, but I must go.

ERIK THE RED: Go then, my son.

NARRATOR: Erik the Red returned to Bratahild, but Leif went on board, followed by his crew. They hoisted sail and headed off into the unknown western sea.

Scene 2: Several days later. In the Atlantic Ocean.

NARRATOR: Guided by the sun and stars, Leif and his men sailed until they spotted land to the west.

VIKING #1: Hail! There is land off to the west.

LEIF: Let us sail in closer. It looks like the land Bjarni saw before reaching Greenland.

VIKING #2: He called it a worthless country. I can see why.

NARRATOR: The men sailed as close as they could, then dropped anchor. They lowered a smaller boat and rowed ashore.

VIKING #1: There are so many glaciers.

VIKING #2: And not a single blade of grass.

TYRKIR: There is one big slab of stone from the glaciers to the sea.

LEIF: Unlike Bjarni, we have been ashore. I will name this place Helluland for what it is, the land of stone slabs.

NARRATOR: Then Leif and his men rowed back to their ship and headed out to sea again, sailing south and west.

Scene 3: Several days later. In the Atlantic Ocean.

NARRATOR: Soon Leif and his men sighted more land.

TYRKIR: Land, again!

LEIF: Let us drop anchor and go ashore.

VIKING #1: This land matches the description of the second place Bjarni saw.

VIKING #2: Yes, flat and wooded, with a white sandy beach.

LEIF: We shall name this place, too. It is a land of forests so I will name it Markland for what it has to offer.

NARRATOR: Anxious to find the final land that Bjarni had seen, Leif and his men hurried back to their ship and set sail.

Scene 4: Two days later. In the Atlantic Ocean.

NARRATOR: Leif and his men sailed for two days, pushed by a north-easterly wind until they again saw land.

LEIF: That is it! That is the land Bjarni described. Let us drop anchor and go ashore.

NARRATOR: Leif and his men rowed to an island north of the mainland. When they walked a little ways onto the island they noticed dew on the grass. Many bent to touch it.

VIKING #1: What is this?

NARRATOR: The men put their hands to their mouths.

VIKING #2: It is the sweetest thing I have ever tasted.

LEIF: Let us go back to our ship and sail into the sound so we can explore the mainland. I can see that this land holds much promise.

ACT III

Scene 1: Late summer, about 1001 A.D. Somewhere in America.

NARRATOR: Leif and his men sailed into the sound. They sailed until their ship ran aground because of the low tide. Then they left the ship and went to explore the land before them.

VIKING #1: Look, up ahead. There is a river.

NARRATOR: Leif and his men sailed the river in a small boat. The river led to a lake. They explored for a while and then turned back toward the sound.

LEIF: Let us go see if the tide has become high enough to bring our ship to anchor in the lake.

NARRATOR: The tide had risen enough to allow Leif and his men to sail the ship up the river to the lake. They carried their supplies off the boat and built temporary huts so that they could sleep on shore. They soon decided to build more permanent lodgings.

LEIF: I think we should spend the winter here. There is much to explore in this new land, and we will be very comfortable.

VIKING #2: We will not lack for food. The river and lake are full of salmon bigger than any I have seen before. And I have seen animal tracks, which means there is fresh meat for the hunting.

TYRKIR: There is no shortage of wood for fuel or building.

LEIF: We could not have found a better spot. Let us build a permanent camp here.

Scene 2: Fall and winter, about 1001–1002 A.D. Somewhere in America.

NARRATOR: Once Leif and his men had finished building their camp, they were ready to begin explorations.

LEIF: I will divide the crew into two groups. One group is to explore the land while the other stays home and looks after the houses.

VIKING #1: How far inland should we explore?

LEIF: You mustn't go so far that you can't get back in the evening. And I want the people in each group to stay together; you mustn't get separated.

NARRATOR: Leif and his men explored all through the fall and into the winter. They found this new land very different from Greenland.

TYRKIR: There is no frost here to wither the grass.

VIKING #2: And the sun shines for hours. The shortest day of the year just passed, and still the sun was up at nine o'clock and did not set for more than eight hours.

VIKING #1: There are many more hours of daylight here than there are in Greenland.

LEIF: That gives us more time to explore this rich land.

Scene 3: Late winter, about 1002 A.D. Somewhere in America.

NARRATOR: It was toward the end of the winter when one of Leif's men made an important discovery on this new land. It happened when Tyrkir became separated from the group. Leif was angry that the men had not stayed together as he had ordered.

LEIF: How could you lose Tyrkir? He is like a father to me! Come. We must find him.

NARRATOR: Leif and twelve of his men had not gotten far in the search when Tyrkir came out of the woods, smiling.

LEIF: Why were you so long, foster-father, and why didn't you stay with the others?

NARRATOR: In his excitement, Tyrkir began speaking his native German. Leif and his men could not understand him.

VIKING #2: Speak so we can understand, friend.

NARRATOR: Tyrkir took a deep breath but could not stop smiling.

TYRKIR: I did not go much farther than everyone else did, but I have some news for you—I've found vines and grapes.

LEIF: Is that true, foster-father?

TYRKIR: Of course it is true! Remember, I was born in a place where there are plenty of vines and grapes. I know them when I see them.

NARRATOR: At this news, Leif and his men were very excited. Grapes did not grow in Greenland, and wine made from grapes was a real luxury. If they could bring back a cargo of grapes along with a load of timber, their journey would have been a profitable one.

LEIF: Tomorrow we will begin gathering cargo for our return journey. We will take turns doing the jobs, felling trees, picking grapes, and cutting vines.

NARRATOR: The men did as they were told. By the time spring came, they had filled the boat with grapes, vines, and wood.

LEIF: It is time to sail back to Greenland. We will share the news that we have found a wonderful place, rich in resources, yet uninhabited by people.

TYRKIR: What will you name this wonderful place?

LEIF: I will name it for what you discovered and what it produces. I will name it Vinland, the land of wine.

⟨ ACT IV ⟩

Several weeks later. Off the coast of Greenland.

NARRATOR: The men kept their eyes on the mountains and glaciers in front of them. They were almost home and could think of nothing but getting there. Then they noticed that Leif was not steering directly for land.

VIKING #1: Leif, why are you holding the ship so hard against the wind?

LEIF: I'll look after the steering all right, but there's something else to look at as well. Can't you see something strange?

VIKING #2: I don't see anything but home.

LEIF: Look again. Is that a ship or a reef?

NARRATOR: The others looked hard where Leif was pointing.

VIKING #1: I think it is a reef.

LEIF: Yes, and there are people stranded on it. Let us sail against the wind so we can get to them. They may be in distress and need us.

NARRATOR: Leif found fifteen men and women who had been shipwrecked on the reef. He rescued them and sailed for home. His foster-father was proud of him.

TYRKIR: After this journey I think you have earned yourself a new name.

LEIF: What is that?

TYRKIR: Leif the Lucky.

LEIF: Of all the new names given on this voyage, I think I like that best.

AFTERWORD

Leif, who did become known as Leif the Lucky, never sailed to Vinland again. Erik the Red died the winter after Leif's return, and Leif took over his father's position of leadership in the community. Other Vikings explored Vinland and some even tried to settle there, but they were not so lucky as Leif. The land was not uninhabited as Leif had thought, and the Native Americans who lived there did not welcome the Viking's presence. Leif's brother Thorvald was killed by a Native American's arrow in Vinland.

BACKGROUND

Who was Leif Eriksson? Leif Eriksson (also spelled Ericson and Eiriksson) was a Viking explorer and the first known European to explore North America. He was born in Iceland about 980 A.D. to Thorhild and Erik the Red. While Leif was a toddler his father was banished from Iceland, discovered Greenland, and established a colony there. Like most young Vikings, Leif probably grew up farming and sailing.

According to the *Greenlander's Saga*, Leif learned about three unknown lands in the west from a merchant named Bjarni Herjolfsson. He chose the 35 best sailors in Greenland to sail with him to investigate these unknown lands. Leif and his men spent the winter in Vinland. They returned to Greenland in the spring with a cargo of logs and grapes, much needed in Greenland. Eventually Leif became one of the leaders of the Greenland settlement. He never sailed to America again.

MAKING CONNECTIONS

Responding to the Play

Vicious Vikings? Ask students what they know about the Vikings. What have they heard about these people? Where did they come from? Why were they feared? Tell students that much of what we know about the Vikings comes from stories written by their victims. Discuss how that might affect our picture of them.

Are you curious? Remind students that when Leif's father and brothers told Leif about Bjarni Herjolfsson's discoveries, they said, "Bjarni was a fool," and "He lacks curiosity." Ask students what they think they would have done if they had been in Bjarni's shoes. Would they have stopped to explore the unknown lands or continued on in search of Greenland? What traits do they think an explorer has that other people might not?

Very superstitious: Point out that Leif's father refused to accompany Leif on his explorations after he fell off his horse, saying it was a bad omen. Ask students if they are superstitious. If so, how? If not, why not? What do they think is the origin of superstitions? Do they truly believe in them?

Hearsay or history: Discuss oral history and the way that the story of Leif Eriksson has been passed down to us. Ask students how much of the story they think we should believe. How important do they think writing is in recording history? Is writing always objective?

Extension Activities

Family saga: Ask each student to choose a favorite family story—the more often told the better—and write it down. After the class shares the stories, discuss how much of the stories they think actually happened and how much has been embellished in the retellings. Compare this with the story of Leif Eriksson's journey to America.

Serendipitous discoveries: Discuss the meaning of the word "serendipity." (*Webster's* defines it as "the faculty of finding valuable or agreeable things not sought after.") Ask students what part serendipity played in Leif Eriksson's voyage to America. (Bjarni Herjolfsson saw the lands only after being blown off course en route to Greenland.) Then divide students into small groups and challenge them to come up with a list of three other explorers. Ask groups to research these explorers to find out what discoveries of theirs, if any, were serendipitous, and have them share their findings with the class.

What's in a name? Ask students if they notice how Leif Eriksson's name relates to that of his father, Erik the Red, and how Bjarni Herjolfsson's name relates to that of his father, Herjolf Bardarson. (The sons' last names are made from the fathers' first names.) Ask students to research their surnames to see if they can find where they came from and what special meaning they may have.

Postcards from the west: Have students make three postcard-size drawings of what, based on the descriptions in the play, they imagine Leif Eriksson saw on his voyage to America. Then ask students to imagine they are members of Leif's crew and have them write a letter home about the journey on the back of each postcard.

ENTERPRISE OF THE INDIES

Christopher Columbus and His Journeys to the New World

CHARACTERS

NARRATOR
COLUMBUS: Italian explorer Christopher Columbus
BARTHOLOMEW: Christopher Columbus's brother
KING JOHN: King John II of Portugal
KING FERDINAND: ruler of Spain

QUEEN ISABELLA: ruler of Spain
SANTANGEL: one of Spain's royal treasurers
SAILORS 1–3
PINZÓN: capain of the *Pinta*
RODRIGO: a young sailor on the *Pinta*

PROLOGUE

Columbus's journey and that of many other European explorers was launched by the quest for a sea route to Asia. Up until 1453, two years after Columbus's birth, Europeans could buy silk, gold, jewels, and spices from the east in Constantinople (now Istanbul, Turkey). This city, located on the long overland trail traders traversed from east to west and back, was a major center of trade between Europeans and Asians for centuries. Then, in 1453, the Ottoman Turks made Constantinople the capital of their empire. They closed the city to their Christian enemies and disrupted overland travel. If Europeans wanted Asian goods, they were going to have to find another way to get them.

READ-ALOUD PLAYS: EXPLORERS Scholastic Professional Books

ACT I

Scene 1: 1484. In a book and map shop in Lisbon, Portugal.

NARRATOR: Christopher Columbus and his brother Bartholomew were looking at a world map in Bartholomew's shop.

COLUMBUS: King John is going about it all wrong. The way to reach the Indies is not by sailing around Africa. It is by sailing west across the Ocean Sea.

BARTHOLOMEW: But no one knows how big the Ocean Sea is. Some men say it is so big it would take three years to sail across it.

COLUMBUS: They are wrong. Look at Ptolemy's map. It shows most of the world covered by land.

BARTHOLOMEW: Perhaps the oceans are much bigger than Ptolemy drew them.

COLUMBUS: No. I am sure Ptolemy's map is right. How could nature be so unorderly as to have more water than land? Also, I have been reading the letters of Dr. Paolo Toscanelli. He says that China is only 5,000 miles west of the Canary Islands. If I sail but half that distance, I should be near the wonders of Marco Polo's Japan.

BARTHOLOMEW: Ah, Cipangu, where whole palaces are made of gold.

COLUMBUS: Yes. And it is my God-given destiny to find a seaward route there.

BARTHOLOMEW: How is that?

COLUMBUS: First, because I was born in Genoa, it is clear that God meant for me to be a sailor. Second, I am named after Saint Christopher, and that makes me a messenger of God. I must go and bring his religion to people in the Indies.

BARTHOLOMEW: You sound quite sure of yourself.

COLUMBUS: I am. I will go speak to King John about my Enterprise of the Indies. I must convince him of the error of his ways and the wisdom of mine.

Scene 2: Later that year. At the king's palace in Lisbon, Portugal.

NARRATOR: Columbus applied for and was granted an audience with the king.

KING JOHN: Speak. What is it you wish?

COLUMBUS: Your Highness, your efforts to find the Indies are misguided. You waste time and money trying to reach the Indies by sailing around Africa. The land of riches can be reached much more quickly by sailing west.

KING JOHN: Who are you, a foreigner, to tell me I am wrong and you are right?

COLUMBUS: Listen to me, your Highness. If you give me ships and money, I know I can find the Indies by sailing west. I know I will find gold there.

NARRATOR: The king conferred with his advisors. They all laughed. The king turned back to Columbus.

KING JOHN: You are a big talker. I cannot give you money based on fancy and imagination. You may go.

NARRATOR: Columbus left the palace disappointed, but not defeated.

Scene 3: 1486. At the royal court in Córdoba, Spain.

NARRATOR: Since King John of Portugal was not interested in his Enterprise of the Indies, Columbus decided to try to gain the backing of King Ferdinand and Queen Isabella of Spain. It took nearly a year for them to receive him.

KING FERDINAND: Speak, servant of the crown.

COLUMBUS: Your Majesties, I propose that the shortest route to the Indies is by sailing west across the Ocean Sea. If you were to sponsor my voyage, you would . . . .

KING FERDINAND (*interrupting*)**:** We are much too busy with affairs of state to take up such a proposal at this time.

COLUMBUS: But if you were to back me on such a journey, you would gain much gold for your crown as well as countless converts to Christianity.

NARRATOR: Columbus directed the latter part of this comment to the queen, an ardent Catholic who insisted everyone in Spain be Christian.

QUEEN ISABELLA: As a fellow Christian you know that right now we are fighting to rid Spain of the Moors, the only remaining Muslims on Spanish soil.

COLUMBUS: I do. And I, too, want to help the cause of Christianity, your Majesty. I will use the riches won on my journey to help recapture Jerusalem from the Muslims.

QUEEN ISABELLA: A noble goal. Let my most learned scholars review your plan. I will give you a small salary. We will talk again when they have made their decision.

COLUMBUS: Yes, your Majesty. Thank you.

NARRATOR: When Columbus hadn't heard from the queen by 1488, he returned to Portugal to petition King John a second time. But, as Columbus reached Lisbon, Bartholomew Diaz sailed into the Tagus River, triumphantly announcing that he had sailed around the southern tip of Africa. Diaz's journey convinced King John that the best way to reach India was by sailing around Africa, not across the Ocean Sea.

Scene 4: Early 1492. At the royal court in Santa Fé, Spain.

NARRATOR: Spain conquered the Moors and drove them out of Granada in January 1492. Now Queen Isabella had time to think of other matters.

QUEEN ISABELLA: I have heard so many opposing opinions about Columbus's proposed Enterprise of the Indies. "The Ocean Sea is not navigable. It is too wide to cross. There is no land on the other side. There are no return winds." But others say that it is all a great unknown. They say that Columbus has as much chance of being right as wrong.

SANTANGEL: My Queen, I agree that there are many arguments against the voyage. But I think that there are more for it. There are great possibilities in the unknown.

QUEEN ISABELLA: So you think I should support it?

SANTANGEL: I think you would be missing a great opportunity if you did not.

QUEEN ISABELLA: I will talk with Ferdinand. Please send for Columbus.

NARRATOR: Columbus arrived at the royal court both pleased and angry. He was pleased that he was finally receiving support for his journey. But he was angry that he had been made to wait so long for it.

QUEEN ISABELLA: Columbus, my council and I are now ready to draw up a contract for your great adventure on behalf of Catholic Spain.

COLUMBUS: It has been a long wait. I wish to be rewarded well for this adventure.

QUEEN ISABELLA: And you shall be.

COLUMBUS: I wish to be knighted and given the title Admiral of the Ocean Sea. I wish to be named Governor and Viceroy of all the lands I might discover, with these titles to be passed down to my sons. I want one-tenth of all the treasure I bring back to Spain.

NARRATOR: Everyone at court was shocked by Columbus's demands.

QUEEN ISABELLA (*angry*): How dare you make such bold requests? You may leave my presence. There will be no contract.

NARRATOR: Columbus walked out of the room. On the way out he spoke to Santangel.

COLUMBUS: Perhaps the king of France will be interested in my plan.

NARRATOR: Santangel hurried to speak to the queen.

SANTANGEL: Do you want the French king to get all those riches?

QUEEN ISABELLA (*shaking her head*): No. Get Columbus back. Tell him we will meet his demands. He will make his voyage in the name of Spain.

⟨ ACT II ⟩

Scene 1: September 1492. On the Ocean Sea (Atlantic Ocean).

NARRATOR: Columbus and 89 others left Palos, Spain, on August 3, 1492, aboard the *Niña*, the *Pinta*, and the *Santa María*. Columbus was captain of the *Santa María*. The ships sailed to the Canary Islands where they replenished supplies and made last-minute repairs to the ships. Then, on September 6, they pulled up anchor and set sail for the Indies.

COLUMBUS: We will take advantage of the winds that blow from the northeast. They will take us to the Indies.

NARRATOR: The trade winds were strong and quickly carried the men out to sea. But within weeks, the men began to get nervous.

SAILOR #1: Columbus is mad. There are no islands out here.

SAILOR #2: If there are, our food and water will be long gone before we find them.

SAILOR #3: And if we are lucky to last until we reach land, that will be our new home, as there are no winds to take us back.

NARRATOR: Columbus tried to reassure his men that they were making good progress and would soon reach the Indies. Then they came to the Sargasso Sea. No one knew what to make of the sea of yellow and green floating weeds. It frightened some of the men.

COLUMBUS: There is nothing to fear. Just keep moving forward.

SAILOR #1: See, he is crazy. He does not even know when to be afraid.

SAILOR #2: He talks about how soft the air is.

SAILOR #3: Perhaps we should show him how hard the water is!

NARRATOR: The three men laughed. They were not the first to think that the best thing to do would be to push their captain overboard. Finally, toward the end of September, there were signs that the ships were nearing land.

SAILOR #1: Look, land birds! Four of them.

COLUMBUS: We are almost there.

NARRATOR: Then, on September 25, the captain of the *Pinta* saw something.

PINZÓN: Look! Look! Land!

NARRATOR: The men climbed up the rigging and looked in the distance. They saw it, too. But it was a false sighting. What they saw must have been clouds on the horizon.

Scene 2: October 10, 1492. On the Ocean Sea (Atlantic Ocean).

NARRATOR: The stress of the long journey and another false sighting were making the men mutinous. On October 10, they demanded that Columbus turn back.

COLUMBUS: We have come to find the Indies and we will find them. Give me three more days and we will have land. If not, we will turn back.

NARRATOR: The crew reluctantly agreed. On October 11, Columbus ordered the ships to sail through the night.

COLUMBUS: Keep your eyes open, men.

NARRATOR: Columbus thought he saw something around ten o'clock that night. He asked one of the sailors on watch if he saw it, too.

COLUMBUS: Look in the distance. Do you see anything?

SAILOR #1: Yes. It looks like a little wax candle.

NARRATOR: Columbus looked again but it was gone.

COLUMBUS: It must have been nothing.

NARRATOR: Then, at two o'clock in the morning, the *Pinta* fired a cannon. One of its crew members was shouting.

RODRIGO: Land ho! Land ho!

NARRATOR: Many of the crew scrambled up the rigging to get a better look. The moon shone down upon white sand cliffs in the distance. Columbus ordered the ships to drop anchor for the night. They would land in the morning.

Scene 3: October 12, 1492. On an island in the West Indies.

NARRATOR: As soon as they landed, Columbus and his men fell to their knees to thank God for their safe journey.

COLUMBUS: I will call this island *San Salvador,* Holy Savior. And I claim this island of the Indies for the king and queen of Spain.

PINZÓN: Congratulations, Admiral.

SAILOR #2: Three cheers for Admiral Columbus!

NARRATOR: When they began to look around, Columbus and his men saw natives standing behind the trees and watching them.

COLUMBUS: Look at the Indians. They are quite as naked as their mothers bore them.

SAILOR #3: Why do they wear no clothes?

COLUMBUS: They are primitive people. They do not know enough to be embarrassed.

NARRATOR: Columbus tried to talk to these people through the interpreter he had brought with him. But the interpreter spoke Spanish, Hebrew, and Arabic, none of which these natives understood. The natives just stood staring at Columbus and his men. In their many layers of clothes, the Europeans looked as strange to the natives as the natives in their state of undress looked to the Europeans.

COLUMBUS: The only gold I see is what they wear on their faces. This is clearly not Japan. We must find a way to ask them where Japan is.

PINZÓN: Perhaps if we can learn where they got their gold nose rings.

COLUMBUS: We will give them some trinkets to win their trust.

NARRATOR: After his men handed out glass beads, red caps, glass mirrors, and small bells, Columbus began his questioning. He pointed to the natives' nose rings and used his hands to ask, Where? The natives made hand gestures back.

SAILOR #1: It is useless. We do not understand each other.

COLUMBUS: Let us go. Cipangu, the place where gold is born, is not here. But I know it is nearby. We will begin exploring these islands tomorrow.

SAILOR #2: We will need guides to help us.

COLUMBUS: Take as many natives as you need.

Scene 4: Fall, 1492. In the Caribbean Sea.

NARRATOR: Columbus and his men spent the next several months exploring the islands in the Caribbean, looking for Cipangu, or Japan, looking for gold. They often thought the Indians were telling them where Cipangu was.

SAILOR #3: Admiral, the natives are saying, "Colba."

COLUMBUS: What? They must mean Cipangu. Ask them to show us the way.

NARRATOR: The natives showed Columbus and his men the way to the island which we now call Cuba.

SAILOR #3: Is this it, Admiral? Is this Cipangu?

COLUMBUS: Of course not, there are no gold palaces. In fact, I am not even sure this is an island. What are the natives saying now?

NARRATOR: The natives were pointing to the interior of the island and saying, "Cubanacan!"

COLUMBUS: What! Kublai Khan! Why, they are speaking of the great leader of China. We must send a party to tell him we are here.

NARRATOR: Columbus sent a group of men into the interior to meet the Great Khan. They returned six days later, their mission a failure. Instead of a palace, all they had found was a village of thatched huts.

COLUMBUS: Let us leave this place and continue our search.

Scene 5: December 24. In present-day Haiti.

NARRATOR: On the night of December 24, Columbus and his crew were anchored in a harbor off present-day Haiti.

COLUMBUS: This time I am certain we are close to Japan. The messengers from the king brought me a belt with a centerpiece of hammered gold. And they said their king was in Cipangu.

SAILOR #1: I thought they said Cybao.

COLUMBUS: They did, but surely they meant Cipangu. Tomorrow will be an exciting day. I must sleep. You keep at the helm. I will see you on the morrow.

SAILOR #1: Yes, Admiral. Good night.

NARRATOR: But the sailor was sleepy, too. He handed the helm over to the ship's boy, reassuring him that nothing could happen on so smooth a sea. He was wrong. The ship grounded on a reef.

COLUMBUS (*shouting*)**:** What is this? What has happened?

SAILOR #1: I just took a short nap, I . . . .

COLUMBUS: The ship! What has happened to my ship?

SAILOR #2: I don't think she can be saved.

COLUMBUS: Try!

NARRATOR: But it was no use. The ship was rapidly filling with water.

COLUMBUS: She is lost! Everyone to the launches. We will go to the *Niña*.

NARRATOR: When they reached the other ship they stood on deck and watched the *Santa María* sink. The next day they salvaged what they could from the ship. A local native chieftain came to offer help and condolences. The latter was in the form of a gold mask.

COLUMBUS: Perhaps the loss of my ship was not a disaster, but great luck. I will leave some men behind to find the gold mine that provided the gold for this mask. Then I will return with more and better ships to collect the gold and bring it to Spain.

NARRATOR: Columbus ordered a fort built for the 39 men who would stay behind. Then, on January 4, 1493, he set sail for Spain. He brought with him some small pieces of gold, "Indians," parrots, and other samples of Indian life. The journey was rough. There were violent storms at sea. Each ship feared the other one lost. But, finally, on March 15, 1493, Columbus sailed the *Niña* into the harbor at Palos, Spain. He sent a letter to the king and queen telling them of his return, and they asked him to come to them at once.

READ-ALOUD PLAYS: EXPLORERS Scholastic Professional Books

⟨ ACT III ⟩

Scene: Spring, 1493. At the royal court in Barcelona, Spain.

NARRATOR: Columbus arrived in Barcelona with a procession of six captive natives, a few caged parrots, and a small sample of gold. He received a royal welcome when the king and queen stood to greet him.

KING FERDINAND: Tell us what you have seen, what you have found.

NARRATOR: As the monarchs listened, Columbus told about his journey. He showed the king and queen the natives, or "Indians," as he called them.

COLUMBUS: These are simple, defenseless people. They ought to be good servants.

QUEEN ISABELLA: What about their religion?

COLUMBUS: I believe they have none. They should easily be made good Christians.

NARRATOR: Columbus also showed the monarchs the birds and the gold.

COLUMBUS: This is just a small sample of all the gold that is to be found there. I left 39 men behind to begin gathering it for us. I will need to have even more ships when I go back to get it all.

KING FERDINAND: We will give you all the ships you need.

QUEEN ISABELLA: This is a good day for Spain, Columbus. You have accomplished much.

COLUMBUS: My trip has been a miracle, your Highness. My life has been a series of miracles.

QUEEN ISABELLA: Ferdinand, would you like to bestow Columbus's titles?

NARRATOR: The king stood and Columbus knelt before him.

KING FERDINAND: We grant you these offices: Admiral of the Ocean Sea and Viceroy and Governor of the islands and mainland you have discovered.

NARRATOR: Columbus basked in the glory of this reception. It was what he had dreamed of all his life. And he still had so many dreams. He would find Cipangu on his next trip to the Indies, he just knew it.

⟨ AFTERWORD ⟩

Columbus made three more journeys across the Atlantic Ocean. He insisted that he had sailed west to find the Indies, and that he'd found them. Columbus died holding strong to that belief.

BACKGROUND

Who was Christopher Columbus? Christopher Columbus was born in 1451 in the Italian port city of Genoa. His father was a wool weaver and his mother was the daughter of a wool weaver. His parents named him for St. Christopher—whose name means "Christ-bearer"—the patron saint of travelers. The eldest of five children, Christopher, like most people of his day, probably had very little formal schooling. Most likely he spent his boyhood helping his father weave, exploring the wharves, watching the boats, and studying the sea. Living by the sea inspired a love for and understanding of the ocean that would last Columbus's whole life.

Columbus settled in Lisbon, Portugal, in 1476, joining his brother Bartholomew in his mapmaking business. While working with his brother, Columbus began to believe he could reach the Indies by sailing west across the Atlantic Ocean. After several years of looking for financial backing for such a voyage, Kind Ferdinand and Queen Isabella of Spain agreed to support his expedition.

After his first voyage, Columbus received a hero's welcome in Spain, despite the fact that he had little to show for his journey except a handful of sick natives, several caged parrots, and a few trinkets of gold. He led two more voyages to the "New World," never finding the gold and spices he was looking for. When he died in 1506, he still believed he had reached the Indies.

MAKING CONNECTIONS

Responding to the Play

A born explorer: Ask students to name the qualities Columbus possessed that allowed him to sail across an unknown ocean. Which of those qualities do the students share? Today, what might someone who has those qualities do with his or her life?

Great possibilities: Reread to students the statement Luis de Santangel made to Queen Isabella, "There are great possibilities in the unknown." Ask if they agree with Santangel's statement. Then ask students to think about a time they did something totally new or different. How did they feel after they did it? What, if anything, did they gain from the experience?

Sail or stay? Ask students if they think they would have signed up to sail on one of Columbus's ships. Why or why not? What things might make a person undertake such a journey?

"A messenger of God": Remind students that Columbus believed he was a messenger of God and that as such he must bring his religion to the people of the Indies. Ask students how this belief helped Columbus win support for his journey. Discuss whether or not students agree with Columbus's goal to convert the Indians to a religion other than their own.

Abusing power: Ask students how Columbus and his men viewed the Indians. How did they treat them? Why did the Europeans think they were better than the Indians? Were they? Does different necessarily mean better or worse? What are some examples of how such prejudice exists today? What can we all do to work against prejudice?

October 12: A day to celebrate? Ask students if they are aware of the controversy over celebrating Columbus Day. Ask students what reasons, if any, they think there are to celebrate the date Columbus landed on the shores of the "New World." What reasons, if any, do they think there are not to celebrate? Discuss the issue and take a vote on whether or not the class thinks the holiday should be celebrated.

Extension Activities

Positive thinking: Ask students to find examples in the play of Columbus's optimism, especially his statement after the burning of the *Santa María*, "Perhaps the loss of my ship was not a disaster but great luck." Discuss the power of positive thinking. Ask each student to write down one or more things that they are unhappy about. Then ask them to try to find a way to look at that negative in a positive light.

Explorer's news: Divide students into small groups and ask each group to write a newspaper article and draw an illustration about certain events during Columbus's first trip to the Indies. Possible topics might be: King John II Refuses Columbus; Queen Isabella Gives Columbus the Go-Ahead; Columbus Sets Sail; Sailors Threaten Mutiny; Land Ho!; The Search for Cipangu; and Triumphant Return to Spain. After they are done, you might want to hang these in a place where students from the whole school can enjoy and learn from them.

Throw him overboard? Remind students how unhappy the sailors on Columbus's ships were. Then divide the class in half and have each side debate whether or not to throw Columbus overboard.

Two worlds meet: Ask students to role play the first meeting between Columbus and his crew and the Native Americans, keeping in mind that the two groups spoke different languages. What are some of the things Columbus and his men might try to say to the Native Americans at their meeting? How would they say it? What are some of the things the Native Americans might try to say to the Europeans? What might each group say among themselves? Give each student a chance to play both an explorer and a Native American.

AN ODYSSEY OF COURAGE

Cabeza de Vaca and His Journey Across America

CHARACTERS

NARRATOR
SAILORS 1–3: men on Narváez's expedition
CABEZA DE VACA: Spanish explorer Álvar Núñez Cabeza de Vaca
NARVÁEZ: Spanish explorer Pánfilo de Narváez
PILOT: a pilot of one of Narváez's ships
TOCOBAGA INDIAN

APALACHEE CHIEF
CASTILLO ⎱
DORANTES ⎬ Cabeza de Vaca's fellow survivors and companions
ESTEBANICO ⎰
AVAVARE INDIAN
ALCARAZ: a Spanish slave trader
PIMA INDIAN

PROLOGUE

On June 17, 1527, under the leadership of Captain Pánfilo de Narváez, five ships sailed from Sanlúcar, Spain, to set up a colony in Florida. King Charles V of Spain named Álvar Núñez Cabeza de Vaca treasurer of this expedition to what Europeans considered the "New World." He also named him provost marshal—putting him in charge of military discipline—and ordered him to keep the official record of the voyage and the colony. It is from this official record, Cabeza de Vaca's *Account*, that we know about the journey and what happened to those who sailed under Captain Narváez once they reached the New World.

ACT I

Scene 1: July 1527. On the Atlantic Ocean.

NARRATOR: Captain Narváez was an adventurer. He did not want to spend a lot of money; he wanted to make a lot of money. So he bought five beat-up ships and crammed them with 600 men and hundreds of animals for his expedition to Florida. He also brought minimal provisions. It was a miserable journey, and the sailors often complained about it.

SAILOR #1: All we eat is bread. I am sick of bread.

SAILOR #2: All the same you must eat it, or you will die. The watery soup and bit of meat or fish that we sometimes get is not enough to live on.

SAILOR #3: I heard that the captain eats cheese, meats, fruits, vegetables, even pastries!

SAILOR #1: Look at it this way. We should be glad there is so little to eat. If we were not thin as masts we could not fit in this boat. As it is, there is barely room to stand, let alone sit.

NARRATOR: Cabeza de Vaca heard these sailors speaking.

CABEZA DE VACA: I know it is difficult now, men. But it will be better in Florida.

NARRATOR: The men did not say anything until he walked away.

SAILOR #2: I hope it is better in Florida.

SAILOR #3: I am beginning to wonder if I even want to continue on to Florida.

NARRATOR: The ships arrived in Hispaniola in late August. One hundred and forty men immediately deserted.

NARVÁEZ: One quarter of my men have run off!

CABEZA DE VACA: I believe many of them were unhappy with the ships' conditions, as well as with the provisions.

NARVÁEZ: I spent a small fortune on this expedition.

CABEZA DE VACA: Yes, Governor. But I believe we should make sure we have ample supplies before heading to Florida.

NARVÁEZ: I have friends in Cuba who will provide me with the men and supplies I need.

Scene 2: October 1527. Cuba.

NARRATOR: The fleet sailed to Cuba. While there, Narváez ordered Cabeza de Vaca and two ships to go to the city of Trinidad for provisions.

CABEZA DE VACA: This is hurricane season, Governor. It is a bad time to sail.

NARVÁEZ: We have no time to waste. It has been four months since we left Spain and it may take us another month to reach Florida. Do as I ordered.

CABEZA DE VACA: Yes, Governor.

NARRATOR: The two ships sailed into Trinidad. Once they had anchored, the pilot of the ship Cabeza de Vaca captained came to speak with him.

PILOT: The winds are picking up, sir, and this harbor offers no shelter. We had better do our business quickly.

CABEZA DE VACA: I will send 30 men into town to bring the supplies back quickly.

NARRATOR: Cabeza de Vaca stayed with the ships while the men went for the supplies. The next day a messenger came to the ship with a letter saying that Cabeza de Vaca had to go sign for the supplies. The captain refused, saying he had to stay with the ship. When another letter was sent later that day, the pilot begged him to go.

PILOT: You must go, sir, if it will hasten the arrival of the supplies. The sooner we are able to load the ships, the sooner we will be able to leave this dangerous place.

CABEZA DE VACA (*sighing*): I will go. But I leave you with these orders. If a hurricane hits, you are to beach the ships and save the people and the horses. Do you understand?

PILOT: Yes, sir.

NARRATOR: Cabeza de Vaca went ashore. By the time he had journeyed inland, the hurricane was in full force. Houses and churches in the village were blown down. Cabeza de Vaca and his men spent the night trying to avoid the wrath of the hurricane. They returned to shore the next morning and found it deserted.

CABEZA DE VACA: I see the ships' buoys in the water, but there is no sign of the ships.

SAILOR #1: There is no sign of them anywhere along the coast.

SAILOR #2: Perhaps they were blown inland.

NARRATOR: The survivors went into the woods and eventually found one of the ship's boats in some trees. Farther inland they found the bodies of two sailors, box covers, a cloak, and a quilt. Nothing else was found.

CABEZA DE VACA: This is a sad day. We have lost sixty men and twenty horses.

NARRATOR: When Narváez came to Trinidad, Cabeza de Vaca told him what had happened.

NARVÁEZ: This news saddens me, but I still wish to go on to Florida without delay.

CABEZA DE VACA: None of the men who survived this hurricane will sail with you, Governor. We wish to spend the winter in a safe harbor.

NARVÁEZ (*annoyed*): Then we will sail to Cienfuegos to wait out this hurricane season.

Scene 3: February 19, 1528. Cienfuegos Bay, Cuba.

NARRATOR: By winter's end, Narváez and his men were anxious to sail for Florida.

NARVÁEZ: We will sail tomorrow. I have found a pilot who has been to Florida and knows its entire north coast.

CABEZA DE VACA: He will be a welcome addition to our expedition.

NARRATOR: They sailed the next day with 400 men, 80 horses, and 5 ships. The first day, the pilot grounded them on a coral reef.

SAILOR #1: This pilot said he knew the way to Florida.

SAILOR #2: Let us hope that he knows the Florida coast better than the way there.

NARRATOR: After 15 days, a storm dumped enough rain to free the ships from the coral reef. The sailing was rough but, finally, on April 12, they sighted land.

SAILOR #1: Land ho! Is it really Florida?

SAILOR #2: At last, we have reached our destination!

CABEZA DE VACA: Let us give thanks.

⟨ ACT II ⟩

Scene 1: April 15, 1528. Tampa Bay, Florida.

NARRATOR: The next morning Narváez took a group of men and rowed ashore. They explored the Indian dwellings they found there.

NARVÁEZ: These lodges are empty. But look!

NARRATOR: Narváez picked a small gold bell up off the ground.

NARVÁEZ: It won't be long before we all have more gold than we know what to do with.

NARRATOR: The next day Narváez raised the Spanish flag and took possession of Florida for Spain. The Indians came out of hiding to see who these strange men were.

NARVÁEZ: I am your new governor. From now on you will obey me. And, as this land now belongs to Spain, you must convert to Christianity, pay taxes, and obey Spanish law.

NARRATOR: Narváez showed them the gold bell.

NARVÁEZ: This is what we come for, gold. Where can we find it?

NARRATOR: The Indians looked from Narváez to the bell. Finally, one of them spoke.

TOCOBAGA INDIAN: Apalachee.

NARRATOR: Narváez and his men continued to find small samples of gold. Whenever they asked the Indians where they found it, the answer was always the same, "Apalachee."

NARVÁEZ: We must go inland to find this place, Apalachee, while the ships sail the coast in search of the harbor that lies farther north.

CABEZA DE VACA: But Governor, we do not have the supplies to make an extensive search of an unknown land. I think we should. . . .

NARVÁEZ (*interrupting*): I have made my decision. We will break camp and leave in search of a better port and better land.

CABEZA DE VACA: I think you are making a mistake.

NARVÁEZ: Fine. Since you so opposed and fear going inland, you should remain and take charge of the ships and the people remaining on them.

32

CABEZA DE VACA: No. No one will ever say I stayed with the ships out of fear. I will go with you on this foolish journey, though I believe you will never see the ships again because you are going inland without preparation.

Scene 2: May 1, 1528. Tampa Bay, Florida.

NARRATOR: Narváez formed a party of 300 men and 40 horses. He ordered the remaining men to set sail for the harbor where they eventually would meet. He expected the entire group to be reunited within a few days, so he gave each marcher only two pounds of biscuit and half a pound of bacon.

NARVÁEZ: To Apalachee!

NARRATOR: The men marched through swamps, lakes, and jungles for weeks, then months. Rather than hunt, the Spaniards killed their horses when they ran out of food. Many men got sick or starved to death during this march. They also met many Indians, some friendly, some not. Whenever they met Indians, Narváez asked the same question.

NARVÁEZ: Where is Apalachee?

NARRATOR: The Indians always pointed the same way: north. Finally, on June 24, they reached Apalachee. They captured the chief and began to ask him questions, using their Indian guides as translators.

CABEZA DE VACA: What is this country like? Is there enough food to eat?

APALACHEE CHIEF: Look around you. You see that we have little food.

NARVÁEZ: But what about the gold? Where is all your gold?

APALACHEE CHIEF: We have no gold.

NARRATOR: Narváez looked at the chief in disbelief. But his own eyes told him they were a poor people.

CABEZA DE VACA: We must go south and look for our ships. We must get back to the sea.

NARVÁEZ: We will begin the journey once our men have recovered.

Scene 3: July 1528. Apalachee Bay, Florida.

NARRATOR: They marched for nine hard days. Disease, starvation, and Indian arrows continued to lessen the Spaniards' numbers. Then they finally reached the sea.

NARVÁEZ: Our ships! Where are our ships?

CABEZA DE VACA: They are not here. We must find our own way off this land.

NARVÁEZ: But how?

CABEZA DE VACA: We must build boats. It is the only way.

NARVÁEZ: You are right. We will build our boats then sail for the nearest Spanish settlement, Pánuco, in Mexico.

NARRATOR: Narváez and his men began to build. It took nearly two months to build five rough, open boats. They made woodworking tools from their weapons, sails from their shirts, and ropes and riggings from horses' tails.

CABEZA DE VACA: Our boats are ready and our food is nearly gone. We must sail.

NARVÁEZ: Let us go. These boats are crude, but they are our only hope.

NARRATOR: On September 22, 242 men on five boats sailed into the Gulf of Mexico. It was hurricane season. Storms washed supplies overboard. The men went for days without food or fresh water. When they stopped to search for food and water, they were attacked by Indians. In late October, they passed the mouth of the Mississippi River. The currents were so strong, the boats became separated. Cabeza de Vaca and his men were carried out to sea.

⟨ ACT III ⟩

Scene 1: November 6, 1528. Galveston Island, Texas.

NARRATOR: After days of being tossed about on the open seas, Cabeza de Vaca's boat was driven ashore by a great wave. Sick and starving, shivering and naked, he and his men soon found themselves surrounded by 100 Indians.

SAILOR #1: They are like giants.

CABEZA DE VACA: Let us offer them gifts.

NARRATOR: Cabeza de Vaca gave the Indians trinkets and bells. In return, each of the Indians gave him an arrow as a sign of friendship.

CABEZA DE VACA: They are friendly. We must ask them for help.

SAILOR #1: Are you sure we can trust them?

CABEZA DE VACA: If we do not ask for help, we will surely starve or freeze to death.

NARRATOR: Cabeza de Vaca tried to speak to the Indians.

CABEZA DE VACA: Will you bring us to your huts?

NARRATOR: The Indians nodded. They led Cabeza de Vaca and his men to their village. The next morning, Cabeza de Vaca learned that one of the other boats had been marooned on the other side of the island. These men soon found their way to Cabeza de Vaca.

CABEZA DE VACA: Captains Dorantes and Castillo! What a wonderful sight. We gave everyone up for lost.

CASTILLO: I do not know the fate of the others. We have survived but, like you, barely.

DORANTES: What do we do now?

CASTILLO: We must resign ourselves to spending the winter here.

CABEZA DE VACA: In the spring we will build new boats.

NARRATOR: It was an awful winter. A terrible illness struck that killed scores of Spaniards and Indians. The Indians blamed the white men for the disease. They threatened to kill Cabeza de Vaca and his 14 fellow survivors. Cabeza de Vaca talked them out of it, saying that if they had power over life and death, they would not have let so many of their own die.

Scene 2: September 15, 1534. South of present-day San Antonio, Texas.

NARRATOR: The men were divided among the different Charruco villages, where most were treated as slaves. Cabeza de Vaca became a trader. He would see the other survivors, who were dwindling in number, during the annual gathering of the Charruco tribes. After six years, there were only four survivors: three Spaniards—Cabeza de Vaca, Dorantes, and Castillo; and Estebanico, an Arab Moor. These four finally escaped in the fall of 1534.

DORANTES: I am tired. We have been running all day.

CABEZA DE VACA: There is smoke up ahead. It is another Indian village.

CASTILLO: But are these Indians friendly? I do not wish to be enslaved again.

ESTEBANICO: I will go ahead and see.

NARRATOR: Estebanico ran ahead, then hurried back.

ESTEBANICO: They are the Avavares. They will welcome us.

NARRATOR: The men were greeted warmly in the village. The Avavares seemed to think the foriegners had special powers, for not long after they arrived, an Indian approached Castillo.

AVAVARE INDIAN: My head hurts a great deal. You must cure me.

CASTILLO (*to his friends*): I am not a healer. What should I do?

DORANTES: Do something, or I am afraid they will turn against us.

NARRATOR: Cabeza de Vaca reached into a bag he had been carrying, pulled out a small handful of a dried herb, and handed it to Castillo.

CABEZA DE VACA: I have seen other natives use this to ease pain. Give it to him to chew on. Then pray over him and make the sign of the cross. God has helped us thus far. He is our only hope.

NARRATOR: Castillo did as he was told. The Indian left but was back a short while later.

AVAVARE INDIAN: You are a healer! My pain is gone.

NARRATOR: News of the healing quickly spread. More people came to be healed. Soon Cabeza de Vaca, Dorantes, and Estebanico were also performing healings.

CABEZA DE VACA: God is doing miracles through us.

CASTILLO: When we heal we are given food. Let us continue to Mexico. If our healing power lasts, we may survive to see our homeland again.

Scene 3: Winter, 1536. The western coast of Mexico.

NARRATOR: The four men continued on their journey, traveling south and west. News of their healing power spread, and they were welcomed at every village. One day they found something that made their hearts soar.

DORANTES: Look at this!

NARRATOR: Dorantes held up a buckle from a sword belt with a horseshoe nail sewn to it.

CABEZA DE VACA: Where did you get it?

DORANTES: An Indian wore it around his neck. He said he got it from bearded men like us, with horses, lances, and swords.

CASTILLO: We must be getting close. Let us continue our journey.

CABEZA DE VACA: And let us give thanks to God.

NARRATOR: The four men continued on their way, often followed by large crowds of Indians who revered them for their healing powers. But the villages they passed were deserted.

CABEZA DE VACA: Why is this country so empty? Where are all the natives?

ESTEBANICO: The bearded men have killed many of them and taken countless others as slaves. Those who escaped are hiding in the mountains.

CABEZA DE VACA: It is wrong that these people should be treated so. If we are to convert them to Christianity and make them subjects of our king, they need to be treated well.

ESTEBANICO: You do not think like most of your countrymen.

CABEZA DE VACA: Perhaps that will change. In the meantime, please tell these people not to fear. Tell them we are looking for the bearded men to tell them not to harm the natives or remove them from their lands.

NARRATOR: The Indians welcomed Cabeza de Vaca's promise of protection. The group that followed Cabeza de Vaca and the others grew.

ACT IV

Scene: March 1536. Near Ocoroni, Mexico.

NARRATOR: Cabeza de Vaca and the others continued to walk south. Finally, in early spring, they heard that there were Spanish soldiers on horseback nearby. Cabeza de Vaca went ahead to meet them and speak to their captain.

CABEZA DE VACA: I am Álvar Núñez Cabeza de Vaca, who sailed with Captain Narváez in 1527.

ALCARAZ: We thought there were no survivors from the inland expedition.

CABEZA DE VACA: There are four of us. The others are following.

ALCARAZ: How did you survive?

CABEZA DE VACA: It was difficult, but we learned much from the Indians.

ALCARAZ: Do not speak to me of Indians! I have not been able to capture any for several days. They are all hiding in the mountains.

NARRATOR: Soon Dorantes, Castillo, and Estebanico caught up with Cabeza de Vaca. Alcaraz barely acknowledged them, he was so busy looking at all the Indians that accompanied them.

ALCARAZ: Here are the Indians I need!

CABEZA DE VACA: We promised these people protection. You are not to enslave them!

NARRATOR: Alcaraz ignored Cabeza de Vaca and spoke to the Indians.

ALCARAZ: We are the lords of the land and you should obey and serve us.

PIMA INDIAN: We do not listen to you, only Cabeza de Vaca.

ALCARAZ: If you listen to him, you must listen to me! We are the same.

NARRATOR: The Indian shook his head.

PIMA INDIAN: My people do not believe that. Cabeza de Vaca and the others heal the sick, you kill the healthy; they are naked and barefoot, you are dressed and on horseback; they give everything away, you steal whatever you can take. We only listen to Cabeza de Vaca.

CABEZA DE VACA: And you would do well to listen to me, too, Captain Alcaraz. Let these people go. Then take us to the nearest Spanish city. We would like to go home.

AFTERWORD

Upon his return to Spain, Cabeza de Vaca asked the king to make him governor of Florida. But the job had already been given to Hernando de Soto. Several years later the king sent Cabeza de Vaca to South America to become governor of Paraguay. His efforts to treat Indians fairly cost him the support of Spaniards. To get rid of him and go back to their cruel ways, they brought false charges against him. Cabeza de Vaca was sent back to Spain in chains. He was imprisoned for several years before being pardoned by the king. Álvar Núñez Cabeza de Vaca died in Valladolid, Spain, in 1557.

BACKGROUND

Who was Álvar Núñez Cabeza de Vaca? Álvar Núñez Cabeza de Vaca was born around 1490 in Jerez, Spain. Cabeza de Vaca was one of the first Spaniards to traverse, on foot, a large portion of the recently discovered territory of North America. He gave us the first written description of a Caribbean hurricane and its aftermath, and was the first European to describe *bison*, or buffalo. He was also a man who cared a great deal for the welfare of the natives of North America, and as such has been compared to the Spanish missionary Bartolomé de las Casas. Cabeza de Vaca died in Valladolid, sometime in 1557.

MAKING CONNECTIONS

Responding to the Play

Law and practice: Tell students that there was a law at the time that Cabeza de Vaca sailed to America stating that no one was to be forced into slavery or made to work for the Spanish against his or her will. Ask students for examples in the play of how this law was obeyed or disobeyed. Then ask why they think the law was flaunted so freely. Discuss the greed of many of the explorers and the physical distance between them and the source of the law. Ask students what they think they would have done if they had been in the explorers' shoes. Would they have obeyed the king's law? How would they have reacted to their peers who didn't? Ask if students have ever been in the position where they were obeying a rule while those around them were disobeying it. How did they feel? What, if anything, did they do about the others' disobedience?

Desert or stay? Discuss with students why 140 men immediately deserted Captain Narváez's expedition when it reached Hispaniola. Ask students what they would have done if they had been on that expedition, deserted or stayed? Ask them to give reasons for their answers.

Fit to lead? Ask students what they think of Captain Narváez. Was he a good or a bad leader? Ask them to find examples in the play to support their answers. Then ask them to brainstorm a list of qualities of a good leader. Who, if anyone, do they know who fits this description?

Foolish pride? Reread the lines in Act II, Scene 1, where Cabeza de Vaca tells Narváez, "No one will ever say I stayed with the ships out of fear. I will go with you on this foolish journey, though I believe you will never see the ships again. . . . " Discuss with students why Cabeza de Vaca went with Narváez, and whether or not they would have done the same if they were he. Then ask students if their pride has ever led them to do something that they later regretted.

Miraculous cures: Ask students how they would explain the healing power of Cabeza de Vaca and the others. Discuss the knowledge that the men must have picked up during their years with different groups of Indians as well as the power of positive thinking.

Alike, but different: Reread the Pima Indian's last lines in Act IV that compare Cabeza de Vaca and his fellow survivors to the Spaniards the Indians have been hiding from. Ask students to compare and contrast Cabeza de Vaca and the slave trader Alcaraz. Challenge students to think about why people like to generalize and put people into groups. How is this helpful and how is it harmful? Discuss the importance of judging people as individuals.

Extension Activities

Storm warning! Reread the description of the hurricane in Act I, Scene 2. Tell students that Cabeza de Vaca gave the first written description of a hurricane. Ask students to write a description of the worst storm they've experienced in their lives, and to draw a picture to accompany it. Share each student's work with the class.

Another point of view: Ask students to imagine they are Tocobaga Indians watching Narváez and his men land near their village. Have them write a diary entry describing this event and their reaction to it, from a Tocobaga Indian's point of view.

Shipbuilding 101: Discuss how Narváez and his men had to use whatever they had to build boats to try and find their way to a Spanish settlement. Divide students into small groups and ask them to build a model boat. Tell them they can use whatever they might find in the classroom, but nothing more. After the boats are completed, have students test them in a tub of water to see which ones stay afloat, and for how long.

Odyssey, the movie: Ask students to imagine this play is being turned into a movie, and to make a poster advertising it. Encourage students to brainstorm a list of actors to play the different parts. The actors can be the students themselves or actual actors.

In defense of the Indians: Tell students that the only Spaniard known to do more and care more for the plight of the Indians than Cabeza de Vaca was missionary Bartolomé de las Casas. Have students research this historic figure and write a brief report discussing his life and beliefs.

CONQUERING LA FLORIDA

Hernando de Soto and His Journey Across America

CHARACTERS

NARRATORS 1 and 2
DE SOTO: Spanish explorer Hernando de Soto
KING CHARLES: Charles I, king of Spain, 1516–1556
ISABEL: De Soto's wife
SCOUT: a scout on De Soto's expedition to *La Florida*

MOSCOSO: one of De Soto's friends
ORTIZ: the expedition's translator
PERICO: a young captive Indian from Napituca
CACICA: the leader of the Cofitachequi
TASCALUSA: the chief of the Atahachi

PROLOGUE

After helping to lead the 1536 Spanish conquest of the Inca Indians in Peru, Hernando de Soto returned to Spain a very rich man. But he was not content to stay home and enjoy his wealth. De Soto's spirit of adventure, lust for greater wealth, and dreams of glory would not let him rest. The "New World," with its promises of adventure, wealth, and glory, beckoned him.

⟨ ACT I ⟩

Scene 1: Spring, 1537. Seville, Spain.

NARRATOR #1: Ever since his return to Spain in 1536, De Soto had been saying that he would like a governorship in the New World. In 1537, he got to ask the king in person.

DE SOTO: Your Majesty, thank you for granting me this audience.

KING CHARLES: I welcome the chance to meet a man of so great a reputation. I have heard marvelous stories of your exploits in the Indies.

DE SOTO: I have been very lucky. My adventures have made me rich.

KING CHARLES: And the crown, as well. What is it you wish to ask me?

DE SOTO: I am not content to sit at home when there is a whole new world to be explored. In the name of Spain, I wish to conquer the unexplored regions surrounding the lands from which I just came.

NARRATOR #2: De Soto wanted to conquer Ecuador, Colombia, and Guatemala.

KING CHARLES: I am pleased with all you have done for the crown thus far. I will speak to my advisors about granting you a governorship in the New World.

DE SOTO: Thank you, your Majesty.

NARRATOR #1: The king consulted his advisors. He was concerned that De Soto might join other powerful rulers in South America and set up their own empire. The king decided to give De Soto a governorship elsewhere in the New World. He sent for the explorer.

KING CHARLES: You will go back to the New World as governor of Cuba and *La Florida*. I want you to conquer, pacify, and populate that vast unknown land.

DE SOTO: I have heard there is a great deal of wealth there, as well.

KING CHARLES: You will send the crown half of any gold, silver, and gems you find. You will convert the heathens to Christianity. And you will build forts and harbors.

DE SOTO: Yes, your Majesty. Thank you.

Scene 2: May 1538. Somewhere in the Atlantic Ocean.

NARRATOR #2: De Soto spent a year preparing for his expedition. It finally left port at Sanlúcar, Spain, on April 7, 1538. More than 700 people—mostly soldiers, nearly all men—set sail on seven ships bound for Cuba. One of the few women who sailed with De Soto was his wife, Isabel. It proved to be a long journey, but Isabel had few complaints.

ISABEL: Some people are concerned that the journey is taking longer than usual.

DE SOTO: There is no need to worry, we will be there soon enough.

ISABEL: I am not worried. I am happy for the time with you. Once we reach Cuba, you will begin preparing for your expedition to *La Florida*. That journey may separate us for a long time.

DE SOTO: Do not worry, you will be very busy while I am gone.

ISABEL: Why do you say that?

DE SOTO: You will see.

NARRATOR #1: De Soto and his fleet of ships arrived in Cuba in early June.

Scene 3: June 1538. Havana, Cuba.

NARRATOR #2: De Soto immediately began preparing to explore and conquer *La Florida*. He bought food, tools, weapons, and small items such as knives, mirrors, and beads to trade with the Indians. He bought horses and hunting dogs. He sent ships to scout the coast of Florida for a good landing port. These sailors returned with good news.

SCOUT: We have found a suitable harbor.

DE SOTO: And the land?

SCOUT: It is full of promise. It is rich and green. And when we showed natives our gold rings, they nodded yes. There is much gold to be found in Florida.

DE SOTO: Of course.

NARRATOR #1: After nearly a year of preparations, De Soto was ready for the journey. He prepared to say good-bye to his wife.

DE SOTO: The ships and the men are finally ready. I have signed my last will and testament. Now there is something I must ask of you.

ISABEL: You know I will pray for you.

DE SOTO: You will do more than that. I am appointing you Governor of Cuba. You will rule in my absence.

ISABEL: But I am a woman, women don't. . . .

DE SOTO (*interrupting*): You have more intelligence and character than most men I know. And I have no doubt of your loyalty to me. You are the new Governor of Cuba.

ISABEL: I will rule as you wish.

NARRATOR #2: Isabel then said good-bye to her husband.

ISABEL: I hope I will not have to rule for too long.

NARRATOR #1: De Soto did not hear his wife's last words. His mind was racing ahead to the ships that awaited him. There were nine in all, with about 600 men, loaded with provisions. On May 18, 1539, De Soto set sail for Florida.

ACT II

Scene 1: May 30, 1539. Tampa Bay, Florida.

NARRATOR #2: De Soto sailed for seven days before sighting land, and five more before making landfall. He knew his first job was to find a suitable campsite.

DE SOTO: Let us march to the north.

NARRATOR #1: De Soto and about 100 of his men marched eight miles through thickets and swamps until they sighted the Indian village of Ocita. The governor sent scouts to explore the village. They quickly returned.

SCOUT: There are about eight huts and they are all empty.

MOSCOSO: Was there any gold?

SCOUT: No. We did not even see any maize.

DE SOTO: There will be plenty of gold later on. For now, this is a suitable campsite. We must move the rest of our people here.

44

NARRATOR #2: It took two days to get all the people, animals, and supplies to Ocita. Once that was done, De Soto dressed in his finest robes and claimed North America for Spain, as Juan Ponce de León and Pánfilo de Narváez had done before him.

MOSCOSO: I would like to see what other Indians live around here, Governor.

DE SOTO: Go, and report back to me.

NARRATOR #1: Moscoso and his men soon met several members of the Timucuan Indian tribe. The Spaniards were startled by the cries of one of the natives.

ORTIZ: Xivilla, Xivilla.

NARRATOR #2: *Xivilla* is the name of a city in Spain. Next, the man made the sign of the cross.

MOSCOSO: Halt! Bring that man to me.

NARRATOR #1: The soldiers grabbed the tanned and tattooed man and brought him to Moscoso, who took a long look at his face.

MOSCOSO: You are Spanish!

ORTIZ: Yes! I am a survivor from the group that tried to rescue Narváez.

MOSCOSO: And these savages did not kill you?

ORTIZ: I escaped the hand of Hirrihigua, who wanted to repay me the cruelty the Spanish had done to him. I found safety with the Timucuan.

MOSCOSO: You are with your own now. You will be of great service to us as a translator.

ORTIZ: I would be honored to work for Spain once more.

NARRATOR #2: When De Soto heard of the Timucuan's kindness to Ortiz, he sent gifts to their chief. The chief accepted them graciously, if nervously. Most of the Indians in the area were unhappy about the Spaniards' arrival. Experience had taught them to expect the worst from these bearded men.

Scene 2: July 1539. Ocita (Florida).

NARRATOR #1: De Soto sent scouting parties inland in search of gold. Within two months, he heard a promising report.

SCOUT: Governor, we have heard of a province called Cale but five day's journey from here. The Indians say the area is rich in gold, silver, and pearls.

DE SOTO: Let us go to this place, for I believe nothing but what I see.

NARRATOR #2: De Soto left 100 men in Ocita to await the return of five ships he was sending back to Cuba for supplies and recruits. Then he took 500 men and left camp in search of riches. The Spanish soldiers crossed swamps and swollen rivers to reach Cale. It was a long, hard journey.

MOSCOSO: Our men are complaining. The travel is difficult in their full armor. And they are hungry.

DE SOTO: I cannot change the geography of this place. But I can find more food.

NARRATOR #1: At the next village, De Soto told Ortiz to ask the chief for food.

ORTIZ: The chief refuses your request, Governor.

DE SOTO: If the chief will not give me what I want, I will take it. And I will punish his people for their inhospitable chief.

NARRATOR #2: De Soto took the food and punished the Indians.

MOSCOSO: Our men are no longer hungry.

DE SOTO: Nor will they ever be, so long as we have arms to take what we want.

NARRATOR #1: After five days, De Soto and his men reached Cale. They did not find the riches for which they had hoped.

SCOUT: There is no gold or silver.

MOSCOSO: But corn and grain are plentiful, Governor.

DE SOTO: Order the men to take as much as we need for three months.

NARRATOR #2: De Soto and his men continued on their journey. They took whatever they wanted—food, slaves, anything—from each village they passed. De Soto's men were tired from the march, especially from fighting off Indians who ambushed them throughout their journey. Finally, on September 15, 1539, they reached the village of Napituca.

SCOUT: Vitachuco, the chief of this village, welcomes us. Our Indian guides say he has prepared a feast for us.

ORTIZ: Wait, Governor! I understand their language and have heard differently. What they plan for us is a surprise attack. You must prepare your men for the ambush.

DE SOTO: My men shall be prepared.

NARRATOR #1: The next day, Vitachuco invited De Soto to review his warriors on a plain outside the village. The warriors had laid down their weapons so that they were hidden in the grass. De Soto and his men followed Vitachuco into the field. Then De Soto raised his arm and shouted.

DE SOTO: Attack!

NARRATOR #2: De Soto and his men killed 40 of Vitachuco's 400 men. Then they continued their journey north. Over the next six months De Soto and his army marched through present-day Georgia and North Carolina, then turned south into Alabama. They continued to rob Indian villages and to be the target of Indian arrows.

Scene 3: April 1540. West of Cofitachequi (South Carolina).

NARRATOR #1: All winter, De Soto and his men asked the natives where they could find gold. They were delighted when a young captive described a land of riches.

PERICO: The country Cofitachequi is near the rising sun. I have heard there is more gold there than anywhere in the world.

MOSCOSO: If that is true, this kingdom offers greater riches than Mexico or Peru.

DE SOTO: Who rules this country?

PERICO: A *cacica*, the cacique is a woman.

MOSCOSO: A woman!

PERICO: Yes. She is very powerful. Many chiefs fear and respect her.

DE SOTO: We fear no one. Let us march east.

NARRATOR #2: De Soto and his army marched. On May 1 they reached the Wateree River, where they were met by a number of canoes. In one of them sat a woman wearing a very long strand of pearls and surrounded by attendants.

CACICA: We have had word of your arrival. Welcome to my kingdom.

NARRATOR #1: As she spoke, the cacica lifted her pearls over her head and handed them to De Soto.

DE SOTO: Thank you, La Señora. Now I shall give you a gift.

NARRATOR #2: With these words, De Soto removed a large ruby ring from his finger and gave it to the cacica.

CACICA: I have sent many of my people to stay elsewhere during your visit, so that you and your people will be comfortable. I will send canoes to bring you across the river.

NARRATOR #1: De Soto and his men were made very comfortable in Cofitachequi. While there was no gold, there were hundreds of pounds of freshwater pearls to satisfy their greed. And the fertile land provided plenty of food to satisfy their hunger.

MOSCOSO: Governor, many of the men are saying they would like to make a settlement here. There are pearls and food and the scouts have found a sea harbor just two days away.

DE SOTO: Have they forgotten their dreams of gold and glory? Have you, Moscoso?

MOSCOSO: No, Governor.

DE SOTO: Good, then let us prepare to leave. I have heard that there is a tribe to the northwest that possesses gold. La Señora will take us there.

NARRATOR #2: The cacica refused to accompany De Soto and his men, so the conquistador took her and several of her people against their will. Then the Spaniards followed their dreams north, into the Appalachian Mountains, becoming the first Europeans to cross this mountain range. When their hard walk did not turn up gold, they turned south.

Scene 4: October 1540. Atahachi (Alabama).

NARRATOR #1: As they marched through present-day Alabama, the Spaniards met a powerful chief named Tascalusa. The chief showed no fear of the Spaniards. He offered them a welcome feast, which De Soto and his men enjoyed.

DE SOTO: Thank you for this splendid feast. Now I must ask that you give us men to carry our burdens and food to bring on our journey.

TASCALUSA: I do not serve others, I am served by others.

DE SOTO (*angry*): I will put you under guard while you think about my request.

NARRATOR #2: The next day, De Soto came to see Tascalusa.

DE SOTO: What do you say to my petition for men and food now?

TASCALUSA: I will give you 400 men as carriers. But I cannot give you food.

DE SOTO: Must I take it?

TASCALUSA: No. I will ride with you to one of my other cities, Mabila, where food is plentiful. There I will give you all that you want.

NARRATOR #1: Secretly, Tascalusa had sent word ahead to Mabila to prepare an ambush. Some of De Soto's scouts heard of it.

SCOUT: Governor, I have seen many men and arms enter the town we are approaching.

MOSCOSO: They are even strengthening the palisade.

DE SOTO: We have nothing to fear. It is the townspeople who will be struck with fear when we march into town on horseback.

NARRATOR #2: De Soto was wrong. When the Spaniards entered the town, they were attacked by thousands of Indians. They quickly escaped as De Soto began shouting orders.

DE SOTO: Surround the palisade. We will break it down.

NARRATOR #1: The Spaniards began breaking through the fortress. The Indians fought back, but the Spaniards had better weapons. After hours of fighting, the Spanish broke through the wall and set the town on fire, thus ending the battle.

DE SOTO: What are our losses?

MOSCOSO: We lost 22 men. Eighty horses and much of our equipment was burned in the fire.

DE SOTO: We will rest until the wounded recover. Then we will continue our march.

NARRATOR #2: While they were still in Mabila, Ortiz came to speak with De Soto.

ORTIZ: Indian captives tell me they have seen Spanish ships in a harbor just 80 miles away. They may be our ships.

NARRATOR #1: De Soto thought about this. He knew that if his army returned to Cuba now, his expedition would be considered a disaster. His men were sick and hungry but, worse, they had found no treasure. They could not go back. De Soto grabbed Ortiz's arm.

DE SOTO: I order you not to tell anyone else about these ships. Do you understand?

ORTIZ: Yes, Governor.

NARRATOR #2: De Soto ordered his men to march north, away from the coast. They wintered in Alibamu. Come spring, they insisted on taking 200 local Chickasaw Indians as porters. The Chickasaw chief launched a secret attack, killing 12 Spaniards and 50 horses, and destroying many of the Spaniards' weapons. De Soto packed up and headed west.

⊰ ACT III ⊱

Scene 1: May 9, 1541. The Mississippi River Valley.

NARRATOR #1: De Soto's men moved slowly now, hampered by hunger, sickness, and injuries. They were beginning to despair that they would never leave the swampy wilderness they marched through.

SCOUT: Governor, up ahead, there is a town surrounded by fields of maize. And in the distance, a great ribbon of water.

NARRATOR #2: De Soto hurried ahead to see for himself.

DE SOTO: That is the great water of which the Indians have spoken. Let us go. We will fill our stomachs and our supply bags at the village. Then we will look at the great water.

NARRATOR #1: De Soto and his men took what they needed from the village. Then they marched to the riverbank.

DE SOTO: We will call this the Great River, the Rio Grande, and claim it for Spain.

MOSCOSO: I wonder what lies on the other side.

DE SOTO: We will sail across and find out.

NARRATOR #2: De Soto and his men chopped trees for lumber to build wooden barges. They crossed the Mississippi on June 18 and spent the next nine months wandering around present-day Arkansas. Wherever they went, they asked for gold. They were always told it was further on. By the following spring, De Soto's men were tired of looking.

MOSCOSO: Governor, we have lost more than half our men, including our interpreter, Juan Ortiz. We have only 40 of the 230 horses we started with.

DE SOTO (*sadly*)**:** It is time to turn back. We will return to the Great River and build boats. Then we will sail down the river to Mexico.

Scene 2: Mid-May 1542. On the banks of the Mississippi River.

NARRATOR #1: By the time the Spaniards reached the Mississippi, De Soto was very sick with fever. He called his officers to his bedside.

DE SOTO: I will not survive this expedition.

SCOUT: But, Governor, you have survived so much.

DE SOTO: I will not survive this. Before I die, I want to thank you for your loyalty despite the hardships you suffered.

NARRATOR #2: The men could not speak.

DE SOTO: I also want to ask your forgiveness for any offense I might have given you.

NARRATOR #1: The scout cleared his throat.

SCOUT: Will you appoint a successor?

DE SOTO: Yes. I appoint my friend Luis Moscoso as my successor.

MOSCOSO: I am honored.

DE SOTO: Please tell the men. And send a priest to hear my confession.

NARRATOR #2: Several days later, on May 21, 1542, De Soto lost consciousness and died. His men worried that the natives would attack if they knew their feared leader was dead. They wrapped De Soto's body in a weighted cloth and, in the middle of the night, sank it in the middle of the Mississippi River.

AFTERWORD

After burying De Soto, Moscoso attempted to march what remained of De Soto's army to Mexico. The Central Texas deserts stopped him, and he turned his army back toward the river. Upon returning to the shores of the Mississippi in 1543, Moscoso and his 350 men built seven crude boats. They sailed these down the Mississippi and into the Gulf of Mexico. Three hundred and eleven survivors finally reached Pánuco, a Spanish settlement in Mexico, on September 10, 1543. During their three-year journey, they had traveled approximately 3,000 miles on land and 1,100 miles on water.

BACKGROUND

Who was Hernando de Soto? Hernando de Soto was born around 1500 in Jerez de los Caballeros, in southwest Spain. His father was an *hidalgo*, a cross between a medieval knight and a country squire. As the second-born son, De Soto would not inherit any of his father's property. He had to make his own way in the world. At 14, the typical age when a boy became a man in that time and place, De Soto left home. He traveled to Seville and, from there, sailed for Central America. There he joined expeditions that explored the tropical rain forests of Panama, searching for treasure and enslaving Indians.

De Soto quickly moved up the ranks of conquistadors. By the time he was in his late twenties, he had gained a reputation as a strong captain and a superb horseman. He had also accumulated a fair amount of wealth, but it was nothing compared to what the next few years would bring. De Soto was second in command to Francisco Pizarro when the Spanish defeated the Inca in 1533. The Spanish explorers' dreams of finding gold were finally met. De Soto returned to Spain a rich and successful man. He eventually returned to North America and traveled thousands of miles through the southeastern part of the present-day United States before dying of fever near the Mississippi River in 1542.

MAKING CONNECTIONS

Responding to the Play

Not content to rest on his laurels: Discuss with students the fact that De Soto was not content to stay home in Spain and enjoy his wealth, fame, and power. Ask students to brainstorm a list of adjectives to describe the kind of man they think De Soto was. Then ask students to imagine themselves in De Soto's shoes. Would they have been content to stay in Spain, or would they have struck out for further adventure?

A fair deal? Reread with students the line at the end of Act I, Scene 1, when King Charles makes De Soto governor of Cuba and *La Florida*. He tells him, "You will send the crown half of any gold, silver, and gems you find." Ask students if they think the king should get half of any wealth De Soto finds. If not, how much, if any, should the king get?

Señora Governor? Ask students if they were surprised when De Soto appointed his wife governor of Cuba in his absence. What do they think this move says about De Soto? What does her response say about his wife? What does it say about the time in which they lived?

Much to criticize: Tell students that Gonzalo Fernández de Oviedo, one of the first historians of the New World, found much to criticize about De Soto's expedition. He said it "caused alteration and desolation of the land and loss of liberty of people, without making Christians or friends." Ask students to look for examples in the play that support Oviedo's criticism.

READ-ALOUD PLAYS: EXPLORERS Scholastic Professional Books

A different outcome? Ask students to imagine that De Soto had been more interested in colonizing than conquering, more interested in founding settlements than in finding treasure. Then ask them, how might the history of the United States have been different under such circumstances? Encourage them to think about how the southeastern United States was eventually settled.

De Soto's legacy: Discuss with students how De Soto's thousand-day expedition through the southeastern United States affected the land and its people. What harm did his expedition cause? Did it cause any good?

Extension Activities

A map of the New World: Divide students into small groups. Ask each group to make a physical map of the area De Soto traversed during his expedition to *La Florida*. Look at the maps together and discuss what it must have been like for an army of 600 men with their animals and supplies to travel through this unfamiliar landscape.

"Picturing" the New World: Tell students that there were no visual records of De Soto's expedition, only written ones. One of the first Europeans to provide a visual record of the New World was the Englishman John White. Ask each student to research John White's journeys to the New World and to hand copy one of the many illustrations he made. Display the illustrations for the whole school to see.

The Seven Cities of Gold: Tell students the tale of the Seven Cities of Gold that De Soto had heard as a child. "Seven bishops and their congregations left Spain after it was invaded by the Moors around 750 A.D. They built boats and traveled west across the Atlantic Ocean. When they reached land, they founded seven cities and filled them with riches." Ask students to write their own legend about a hidden treasure. Encourage them to fill their legends with enough facts to make them plausible, so someone like De Soto would be willing to set off in search of the treasure.

De Soto and the Incas: Ask students to research and write about De Soto's role in conquering the Incas of Peru. Have them include in this report a comparison of De Soto's early conquest with his expedition to *La Florida*.

SEARCHING FOR THE FATHER OF WATER

 ## Sieur de La Salle and His Explorations of the Mississippi River

CHARACTERS

NARRATOR

LA SALLE: French explorer René-Robert Cavelier, Sieur de La Salle

FRONTENAC: Governor of New France, 1672–1682

EXPLORERS 1 and 2

TONTI: La Salle's assistant

ILLINOIS CHIEF:

KING LOUIS: King Louis XIV, ruler of France, 1638–1715

NIKA: a Shawnee Indian guide

CAPTAIN BEAUJEU

JOUTEL: La Salle's friend and lieutenant on his final expedition

CAVELIER: La Salle's brother, Abbé Jean Cavelier

MORANGET: La Salle's nephew

LIOTOT: member of La Salle's final expedition

DUHAUT: member of La Salle's final expedition

PROLOGUE

René-Robert Cavelier, Sieur de La Salle, sailed to New France (Canada) in 1667. He became a prosperous farmer and fur trader. But prosperity alone was not enough for La Salle. The many Indians he befriended told La Salle of a great river, "the father of water," that emptied into the sea. When he learned that Louis Jolliet and Jacques Marquette had explored the upper regions of this river, the Mississippi, La Salle began dreaming of exploring the river all the way to the sea. With the approval of King Louis XIV, La Salle began preparing for this expedition in the summer of 1678.

⟮ ACT I ⟯

Scene 1: Late summer, 1678. Montreal.

NARRATOR: La Salle spoke with his friend and supporter about his planned expedition.

LA SALLE: Governor, the king has granted me permission to explore the great river to its mouth and to set up forts all along the way.

FRONTENAC: Is the king paying for your expedition?

LA SALLE: No, I will have to find my own funding. But he has granted me a monopoly on buffalo hides that will repay my debt once the voyage is over.

FRONTENAC: Is there anything I can do to help?

LA SALLE: Your good word will help me secure the credit I need to finance my voyage.

FRONTENAC: You have it.

LA SALLE: Then I will begin to build the first European ship that will cross the Great Lakes. I will call it *Griffon*, for the animal on your coat of arms.

FRONTENAC: I am honored. Have you chosen who will build this ship?

LA SALLE: Yes, I have chosen master carpenters, pilots, and ironworkers. And to lead them I have hired a very able young man, Henri de Tonti.

NARRATOR: La Salle sent Tonti and his men to the Niagara River, near present-day Buffalo, New York, to begin building the 45-ton sailing vessel. He raised money and gathered the supplies he needed. When the *Griffon* was ready in the summer of 1679, the crew moved it to Lake Erie, where La Salle boarded it and raised the ship's sails.

Scene 2: January 1680. On the shores of the Illinois River.

NARRATOR: La Salle and his men sailed the length of Lakes Erie and Huron in the *Griffon*. Then they sent the *Griffon* back filled with furs to sell. La Salle hoped to use the money to repay some of his debts. They continued searching for the Mississippi on foot. Eventually La Salle learned that the *Griffon* never arrived. In early January, the cold and miserable explorers arrived at a large village of Illinois Indians near present-day Peoria, Illinois. La Salle, who had learned to speak a number if Indian dialects during his years in New France, greeted the Illinois Indian chief.

LA SALLE: We come as friends and bring you gifts.

ILLINOIS CHIEF: Come. We will have a feast to celebrate our new friendship.

NARRATOR: During the feast, La Salle made a proposal to the Illinois chief.

LA SALLE: We would like to build a fort nearby. We will be able to trade with you and protect you from the Iroquois.

NARRATOR: The Illinois chief didn't like La Salle's proposal. He had heard that La Salle and his men were spies for the Iroquois. Even after La Salle dispelled that rumor, the chief did not want the French around. So he began to tell stories to scare them away.

ILLINOIS CHIEF: The Mississippi River is crawling with giant lizards and serpents. They are the only ones who escape the river's mighty whirlpools.

NARRATOR: The chief's words scared off six of La Salle's men, and led several others to try to poison their leader. But La Salle would not be stopped. He built a fort and named it Fort *Crèvecoeur,* which is French for "heartbreak."

LA SALLE: We will also build a new ship to sail to the Mississippi in the spring.

NARRATOR: By late winter, La Salle knew he would have to go back to New France for supplies. He left Tonti in charge. Then he, four other Frenchmen, and the Indian guide, Nika, set out on the long journey back to Fort Frontenac on March 1, 1680.

Scene 3: May 6, 1680. Fort Frontenac.

NARRATOR: It was a long and difficult journey. The hungry and cold men had to keep a constant lookout for hostile Iroquois. They finally reached Fort Frontenac on May 6.

NIKA: We have made it.

LA SALLE: We must go on to Montreal, where I can get money and supplies.

NARRATOR: In Montreal, La Salle learned that the *Griffon* had vanished. He tried to put this bad news behind him as he paid off creditors and gathered the supplies he needed. Within a week, he was heading back to Fort Frontenac. He received more bad news there when two French fur traders handed him a letter from Tonti.

LA SALLE: This cannot be! The men have destroyed Fort Crèvecoeur! Now they are coming to kill me!

NIKA: What will you do?

LA SALLE: I will arrest them!

READ-ALOUD PLAYS: EXPLORERS Scholastic Professional Books

NARRATOR: La Salle surprised and arrested his would-be assassins on the shores of Lake Ontario. Then he went looking for Tonti. After nearly a year of searching, La Salle found his friend safe with the Potawatomie Indians near Mackinac. The two men returned to Montreal. La Salle was disappointed, but not defeated. He would try again.

ACT II

Scene 1: Late fall, 1681. Montreal.

NARRATOR: Once back in Montreal, La Salle met with his friend, the governor.

FRONTENAC: What will you do next?

LA SALLE: I will mount another expedition. This time I will bring more Indians. I have already asked several Abenaki and Mohican Indians to travel with me.

FRONTENAC: So you are already planning your next expedition?

LA SALLE: Of course. What did you expect?

NARRATOR: When La Salle left on his journey, he did so in the company of 18 Indian hunters and guides, their wives and children, and 22 Frenchmen.

Scene 2: February 1682. The Illinois and Mississippi Rivers.

NARRATOR: La Salle's expedition began sailing down the Mississippi on February 13. They sailed past where the Missouri empties into the Mississippi from the west, past where the Ohio empties into the Mississippi from the east. On February 24, La Salle ordered the canoes ashore near present-day Memphis, Tennessee.

LA SALLE: This looks like a good place to hunt for food.

NARRATOR: Many of the men went off to hunt. One of them, a Frenchman named Pierre Prudhomme, did not return.

EXPLORER #1: Prudhomme has not returned from the hunt.

LA SALLE: Organize a search party to find him.

NARRATOR: While several men looked for Prudhomme, La Salle built a small fort. Prudhomme wandered back to camp six days later, embarrassed at having gotten lost.

LA SALLE: You are safe! I will name this place Fort Prudhomme!

NARRATOR: After naming the fort after him, La Salle left Prudhomme in charge of a small group of soldiers he stationed there. Then the expedition continued down the Mississippi, nearing the mouth of the Arkansas River in early March.

TONTI: I think we have traveled as far as Marquette and Jolliet.

EXPLORER #2: We will be the first Europeans to see this part of the river.

LA SALLE: We cannot see anything at all with the fog that is settling in!

EXPLORER #1: We may not be able to see, but I hear the steady beat of drums.

TONTI: And, if I am not mistaken, the cries of a war dance.

LA SALLE: Let us cross to the opposite shore.

NARRATOR: La Salle and his men landed on the opposite shore and quickly built a fort to protect themselves. When the fog lifted, a group of Indians shot a single arrow at them.

LA SALLE: Wait! Do not shoot back. We want them to know we come in peace.

NARRATOR: In this way, La Salle befriended the Quapaw Indians. As he continued on his journey, La Salle also befriended the Taensa and the Natchez Indians. La Salle enjoyed making these friendships, but his mind never strayed from his goal: reaching the mouth of the Mississippi. On April 6, it appeared he was close to reaching that goal.

LA SALLE: The current is slow and the water is salty, we must be nearing the sea.

TONTI: Look, up ahead. The river flows into three branches.

LA SALLE: We will divide into three groups to explore each branch.

NARRATOR: The groups only had to sail for several miles before reaching the sea.

EXPLORER #2: The sea, at last!

TONTI: This must be the Gulf of Mexico.

LA SALLE: At last!

NARRATOR: The entire party went ashore near present-day Venice, Louisiana. La Salle built a monument. He raised a large cross and a post that bore the arms of the royal family.

TONTI: Let us raise our muskets in honor of this great event.

NARRATOR: The men fired their muskets. La Salle asked the priest to lead the group in prayer. Then he spoke the words he had rehearsed in his head for years.

LA SALLE: In the name of Louis the Great . . . I . . . do now take . . . possession of this country of Louisiana, the seas, harbors, ports, bays, . . . all the nations, peoples, provinces, cities, towns, villages . . . and rivers . . . from the mouth of the great river St. Louis . . . also along the . . . Mississippi, and the rivers which discharge themselves therein . . . as far as its mouth at the sea, or Gulf of Mexico.

NARRATOR: La Salle had claimed half of the North American continent for France. Now he had to feed his people. There was little to eat at the Gulf except alligator meat. So they climbed back in their canoes and began their journey upriver, back to Canada.

ACT III

Scene 1: Spring, 1684. The royal palace at Marseilles, France.

NARRATOR: When he returned to New France, La Salle found Frontenac gone and a new governor, La Febvre de La Barre, in his place. When La Barre refused to support La Salle in further expeditions, the explorer returned to France to appeal to the king.

LA SALLE: Your Highness, I have many enemies in the New World and the old. They do not want me to continue the work I do for you and my country.

KING LOUIS: I know you wish to do more and there is more I wish you to do. I would like you to set up a permanent colony at the mouth of the Mississippi. Such a colony may help us take control of the Gulf of Mexico from Spain.

LA SALLE: I am honored to do as you ask.

KING LOUIS: I hereby name you viceroy of North America and supreme commander of the next expedition. My colonial minister will work out the details of the expedition.

LA SALLE: Thank you. I will be awaiting your orders.

NARRATOR: The king chose a captain in the royal navy to command the ships of the expedition. La Salle asked his brother, Abbé Jean Cavelier; two teenage nephews; his Indian guide, Nika; and Henri Joutel, a friend, to make the journey with him.

Scene 2: July 24, 1684. Port La Rochelle, France.

NARRATOR: On July 24, 1684, four ships carrying more than 300 people set sail from La Rochelle, France, to establish a colony in Louisiana. La Salle and the Sieur de Beaujeu, the captain of the expedition, took an immediate dislike to each other.

CAPTAIN BEAUJEU: If I am to lead this expedition, you must tell me where I am going.

LA SALLE: I am leading this expedition.

CAPTAIN BEAUJEU: I have full authority over this fleet while it is at sea.

LA SALLE: I will let you know our exact destination when I am ready. Meanwhile, continue sailing west.

NARRATOR: La Salle's reluctance to give Beaujeu directions was caused by more than his irritation at having someone else in charge. It was also caused by his lack of knowledge about the geography of the Gulf of Mexico. He had never sailed there on the open seas.

CAPTAIN BEAUJEU: We will dock in the Indies. Then you must give me directions.

NARRATOR: On September 25, Beaujeu anchored the *Joly* at Santo Domingo. The supply ship, the *St. François*, was captured by Spanish pirates. The *Amiable* and *La Belle* made it safely to port, but La Salle was devastated over the loss of his supply ship. He became very ill. He was not well enough to resume the journey until late November.

CAPTAIN BEAUJEU: Now you must tell me where I am to sail.

LA SALLE: Your maps will lead you to the Gulf of Mexico. Once there, I will direct you to the mouth of the Mississippi.

NARRATOR: The ships arrived in the Gulf of Mexico in late December.

CAPTAIN BEAUJEU: We will stay near the coast so you can tell me where to land.

NARRATOR: After sailing along the southern coast of North America for two weeks, La Salle told Captain Beaujeu to drop anchor. They were in Matagorda Bay—about 400 miles west of the mouth of the Mississippi River.

Scene 3: January 20, 1685. Matagorda Bay.

NARRATOR: La Salle must have realized that he was not at the mouth of the Mississippi River, but he decided to try to make the best of things. He led his people ashore.

LA SALLE: We will camp here until we find the Mississippi.

NARRATOR: While he spoke, several settlers wandered off the beach and into a band of local Indians. They began to fight. One of the explorers ran to La Salle for help.

EXPLORER #1: Viceroy, you must help us. There are dangerous Indians.

NARRATOR: La Salle went to settle the dispute. While he was gone, the *Amiable*, which carried most of the expedition's remaining supplies, ran aground. La Salle returned to a horrible scene at the beach.

LA SALLE: Can anything be rescued?

JOUTEL: We will do what we can.

NARRATOR: But a terrible storm broke during the salvage operation. In the end, most of the ship's tools, weapons, food, and medicines were lost. The only thing that could be saved was the ship's lumber, which was used to build their settlement, Fort St. Louis.

JOUTEL: We will starve if we do not get more food.

LA SALLE: Captain Beaujeu is returning to France on the *Joly*. He will ask the king to send us more supplies.

NARRATOR: Captain Beaujeu sailed for France. Months passed. La Salle led small parties in search of the Mississippi. The settlers struggled to survive and waited, in vain, for help from France.

JOUTEL: It has been many months and the king has not sent help.

CAVELIER: I am afraid we are on our own.

LA SALLE: We will keep searching for the Mississippi. We will be fine.

NARRATOR: But they were not fine. Settlers were dying from sickness, starvation, and Indian attacks. When the last ship, *La Belle*, ran aground in March 1686, many lost hope.

JOUTEL: We have no ship to carry us back to France, no way to send for help.

LA SALLE: I must find the Mississippi. Then I can sail to Canada for help.

Scene 4: March 1687. Near present-day Navasota, Texas.

NARRATOR: La Salle and about two dozen men left Fort St. Louis on January 7, 1687. They marched east in search of the Mississippi. The weather was harsh. The men hunted, but were often hungry. Hunger and cold made many men short-tempered. In mid-March, after crossing the Trinity River, La Salle decided they needed to rest.

LA SALLE: Let us set up camp here. We will send out a hunting party.

NARRATOR: Nika led the hunting party, which killed two buffalo several miles away from camp. Then he made the long walk to get help in carrying the buffalo back to camp.

NIKA: Viceroy, we need help bringing back the buffalo.

LA SALLE: My nephew Moranget is young and strong. He will help you.

NARRATOR: Nika returned to the buffalo with Moranget. The other hunters had already begun carving up the buffalo.

MORANGET: You should have waited for me to prepare the carcasses.

LIOTOT: There is nothing wrong with the way we prepared the carcasses.

MORANGET: It appears to me that you have taken the best parts for yourself.

DUHAUT: You are like your uncle, full of useless talk!

MORANGET: I will tell my uncle what you said when we get back to camp tomorrow!

NARRATOR: Moranget walked away with Nika to find a good sleeping spot.

DUHAUT: Moranget will not get the chance to tell his uncle what I said.

NARRATOR: That night, while Moranget slept, Liotot and Duhaut murdered Moranget with an ax. They also murdered Nika and La Salle's servant.

LIOTOT: La Salle will surely murder us if he finds out what we've done.

DUHAUT: Not if we get to him first. I am sure La Salle will come looking for his nephew.

NARRATOR: When the men did not return to camp, La Salle became concerned. On March 19, he set out to find them with a priest from his traveling party.

LA SALLE: I feel a profound sense of sadness, Father. I hope the men are unharmed.

NARRATOR: When they heard La Salle approaching the hunting spot, Liotot and Duhaut hid in the bushes. When La Salle was near enough, Duhaut shot and killed him. La Salle was 43 years old.

AFTERWORD

Six men, including Jean Cavelier and Joutel, reached Montreal in the summer of 1688. They were too late to send help to Fort St. Louis. Indians had murdered nearly everyone left in the settlement. The few they took as prisoners were later captured by the Spanish.

BACKGROUND

Who was Sieur de la Salle? René-Robert Cavelier was born in Rouen, France, on November 21, 1643, into a wealthy family dominated by business and religion. La Salle, who took this part of his name from a family estate given to him by his father, attended schools run by Jesuits and studied to become a priest. One of the things that appealed to him about this missionary order was that its members traveled all over the world to do their work. In the end, however, he could not wait to finish his training to begin his travels. He left the order and sailed to Canada in 1667 for what he hoped would be a life of adventure.

He began exploring the interior of North America in 1669, eventually traveling to the mouth of the Mississippi River, building forts and claiming land for France along the way. Upon his return to France, he was named viceroy of North America.

His final trip to America ended in disaster. His expedition traveled to the Gulf of Mexico, looking for the mouth of the Mississippi. They sailed 400 miles past it, and finally dropped anchor in Matagorda Bay, in present-day Texas. La Salle often pushed his men to the point of rebellion, and on March 20, 1687, he was ambushed and murdered by two of his men. The explorer was not yet 44 years old.

MAKING CONNECTIONS

Responding to the Play

Try, try again: Ask students to think of some of the many setbacks La Salle encountered on his journeys. Ask what this says about La Salle as a person that he persevered despite these setbacks. Would they like La Salle as a leader? As a friend? As an employee? Discuss.

Good relations: Ask students to look for examples of how La Salle treated the Indians. Ask students why they think his relations with the natives were generally good. How important do they think good relations with the Indians would be in exploring and settling a region?

Fort Heartbreak: Remind students that *crèvecoeur* means "heartbreak" in French. Ask them why they think La Salle named his Illinois fort Crèvecoeur. How did the fort truly live up to its name?

Betrayals: Discuss with students the many times La Salle's men betrayed him. Ask them if they think that a leader plays any part in his or her followers' betrayals. If so, what? What reasons, if any, can they think of for La Salle's followers to betray him? Do they think they would have been loyal to La Salle or would they have betrayed him? Why?

Lost: Ask students what, if anything, they think La Salle could have done differently when trying to establish a French colony at the mouth of the Mississippi. Do they think the colony failed because of bad luck, bad leadership, or a combination of both? Ask students to explain.

"A life of honor": Read these words of La Salle's to your students, then discuss: "The life I am leading has no other attraction for me than that of honor; and the more danger and difficulty there is in undertakings of this sort, the more worthy of honor I think they are." Ask students, based on his own words, if they think La Salle was happy with his life. Ask students to explain.

Extension Activities

On the cover: Ask students to draw an illustration for the cover of a book about La Salle's life. Display these illustrations in a place where the entire class can see them.

Mystery of the *Griffon*: Ask students to write a brief story describing what they think happened to La Salle's sailing ship, the *Griffon*. Have students share their stories with the class.

Mississippi River research: Divide students into small groups. Ask each group to do a research project on one aspect of the Mississippi River. Research areas might include geography, commerce/transportation, flooding, animal and plant life, history, and literature. Projects could include anything from time lines to dioramas, topographical maps to charts, and even skits. Have each group share what they learned and present their projects to the rest of the class.

Talking history: Ask students to choose a scene from the play and expand upon it. For example, ask them to imagine the scene when La Salle's men rebelled and destroyed Fort Crèvecoeur before setting out to kill him. What do they think led up to that? Have students write down and, later, perform imaginary dialogue from that scene or any other of the play's scenes they choose to expand.

Last words: Ask students to imagine they are working for a French newspaper when they receive word of La Salle's death. Have each of them write a brief obituary recounting this man's life and accomplishments.